Other Books by Jean Fritz

AND THEN WHAT HAPPENED, PAUL REVERE?

CAN'T YOU MAKE THEM BEHAVE,
   KING GEORGE?

GEORGE WASHINGTON'S BREAKFAST

SHH! WE'RE WRITING THE CONSTITUTION

WHAT'S THE BIG IDEA, BEN FRANKLIN?

WHERE DO YOU THINK YOU'RE GOING,
   CHRISTOPHER COLUMBUS?

WHERE WAS PATRICK HENRY ON THE
   29TH OF MAY?

WHY DON'T YOU GET A HORSE, SAM ADAMS?

WILL YOU SIGN HERE, JOHN HANCOCK?

Will You Sign Here,

by Jean Fritz
pictures by Trina Schart Hyman

Penguin Putnam Books for Young Readers

Text copyright ©1976 by Jean Fritz
Illustrations copyright © 1976 by Trina Schart Hyman
All rights reserved. This book, or parts thereof, may not be reproduced in
any form without permission in writing from the publisher. PaperStar and
G. P. Putnam's Sons are divisions of Penguin Putnam Books for Young Readers,
345 Hudson Street, New York, NY 10014.
PaperStar is a registered trademark of The Putnam Berkley Group, Inc.
The PaperStar logo is a trademark of The Putnam Berkley Group, Inc.
Originally Published in 1976 by Coward McCann, Inc.
First PaperStar edition published in 1997.
Published simultaneously in Canada.
Manufactured in China

Library of Congress Cataloging Publication Data
Fritz, Jean. Will you sign here, John Hancock?
SUMMARY: A biography of the first signer of the Declaration of Independence
outlining all that he did for himself as well as what he did for Massachusetts
and his new nation. 1.Hancock, John, 1737-1793—Juvenile literature.
[1. Hancock , John 1737-1793. 2. United States—History—Revolution,
1775-1783—Biography] I. Hyman, Trina Schart. II. Title.
E302.6H23F74 1976 [92] 75-33243
ISBN 0-399-23306-7 (hardcover)
15 17 19 20 18 16
PaperStar ISBN 0-698-11440-X (paperback)
13 15 17 19 20 18 16 14 12

To Anne, Ellen, and Dana.

In the days when Boston was the biggest city in America there were in the south end of town 45 acres of land set aside as a Common for the use of all. There were pastures for Boston's cows, training fields for Boston's soldiers, a shaded walk for Boston's lovers, 3 ponds for Boston's frogs and on the west edge of the Common there was a wishing stone. Anyone who cared to could run around the stone nine times and then stand on it and make a wish.

Of all the boys in Boston, John Hancock lived nearest to the stone. Ever since he'd been seven years old and his father died, he had lived with his Uncle Thomas and his Aunt Lydia in their house on the west edge of the Common. No one knows whether John used the stone or not. After all, what would he wish for? He lived in a house so large it had 54 windows, he had a rich and loving uncle, splendid clothes, a crimson curtain around his bed, plum-cake to eat whenever he wanted it, and horses standing in the stable at his pleasure. Of course, for all we know, he had so much *because* he ran around the stone. Perhaps he ran himself dizzy. On the other hand, as time went on, John Hancock made some grand wishes and perhaps he should have run more.

Actually, what John Hancock wanted most was for people to like him. Not just some people. *Everybody.* It wasn't hard to like him. He was nice-looking, friendly, kind, generous, and he gave fantastic parties. But he wanted people to like him so much that they would elect him to offices. He wanted to march at the head of parades, to sit in the seat of honor, and to stand on the center of platforms. Of course, to be popular, he had first to be noticed. And he was noticed. John Hancock dressed in the richest, flashiest clothes he could find. When he was still a young teen-ager at Harvard College, he had a scarlet coat that attracted so much attention that a doctor from a neighboring town hiked 30 miles for a piece of cloth to make a coat like John's. Generally, John's waistcoats were of embroidered satin, his breeches were of velvet, and his shoes had gold or silver buckles on them. He liked a touch of lavender or purple about him and he was wild about lace—gold lace dangling from his cuffs, gold lace dripping down his shirtfront.

Sometimes his Uncle Thomas worried about John's extravagance. Once in a letter he scolded him. John was in London at the time. He was 24 years old and for the last 6 years he had been working for his uncle in his mercantile business. After the scolding John wrote back:

"I am not remarkable for the plainness of my dress," he admitted, "and can't say I am without lace . . . I find money, some way or other, goes very fast."

Money always went fast for John, but in 1764 his uncle died and suddenly there was more money. John inherited his uncle's fortune and at 27 years old, he was the richest man in New England, the second richest in America. If people hadn't noticed him before, they noticed him now. Certainly Samuel Adams noticed. These were the days when England was starting to make trouble for America, and Samuel Adams, who would have liked nothing better than to knock England right off the map, was looking for men to help his cause. And who could be more helpful than John Hancock with his winning ways and his large pocketbook?

So Samuel Adams became John's friend. He praised John, took him to meetings, put him on platforms, and saw that he was elected to his first public office. John was a selectman now and decided that he needed a servant to help him dress. He sent to London and in due time, back came Frank, a servant who knew all the ins and outs of dressing. Frank kept John's clothes cleaned, his buckles polished, his wigs curled, his buttons sewed on, and every morning he asked John what he wished to wear.

Once he was dressed, John would go to his warehouse near the dock where his ships loaded and unloaded. He owned or held interest in 20 ships. When his ships sailed out of Boston, they carried whale oil, whalebone, codfish, and lumber; when they sailed back, they brought cloth, tea, paper, hardware, books, furniture, ribbons, buckles, fans, wine, salt, leather, lime, and swords. And news. There was always news from London when a ship came into port.

In 1765 the news was bad. England had enacted the Stamp Act, imposing taxes on Americans in 55 different ways. Americans, who had always managed their money in their own assemblies, considered the act *unconstitutional*. Naturally they were furious. John Hancock, too. He said there was nothing or no one on earth that could make him pay a penny of that "damned tax." He said it often and loudly. Once, at a dinner for members of Samuel Adams' Patriot Party, he said it so well that he was cheered. Huzza! Huzza! Huzza! John had never been huzzaed before and he was so pleased that he almost huzzaed himself.

14

The next year the news was good. England repealed the Stamp Act. The news was brought to Boston in John Hancock's brig the *Harrison*, and John announced it to the public.

Such news called for a celebration, and who was the Number One Celebrator?

John Hancock, of course. He festooned his house with flags, piled his tables high with food, lighted up his windows (all 54 of them), and when the townspeople gathered on the Common, John Hancock threw open his doors for one of the grandest parties Boston had ever had. For those who couldn't fit in the doors, he rolled out a 126-gallon cask of Madeira wine. Then he set off fireworks—huzza! huzza! Rockets in the air, "beehives" and "serpents" on the ground.

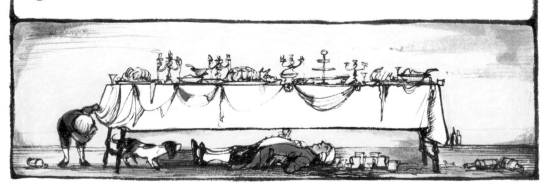

John was so popular now that he was one of Boston's four representatives to Massachusetts' governing body. When he went out, he rode in one of his 9 conveyances. He had an elaborate coach with four wheels and his coat of arms emblazoned on the door. He had both a large and small chariot (four wheels but less grand than a coach), a chaise (a two-wheel carriage for two), a sulky (a two-wheel carriage

16

for one), a kittereen (a two-wheel carriage with movable hood), a booby-hut (an enclosed sleigh), a double sleigh, and a single sleigh. And they were all painted bright yellow. Sometimes when he went out, small boys ran alongside; sometimes he stopped and gave them coins. John Hancock loved to give presents: wood to the poor, steeples to churches, books to libraries. Indeed, if he felt he wasn't getting enough attention, he often gave the town a gift.

They were not mean gifts. Once he gave Boston a fire engine. Once a concert hall. Once a row of lime trees for the Common. Once a bandstand. After each gift, he was huzzaed, and with each huzza, John warmed and swelled, like an apple rounding, reddening, ripening in the sun.

Still, not everyone liked John.

King George of England didn't like him. He didn't like the way John had acted during the Stamp Act, and when England tried again (in 1767) to tax Americans and when John still wouldn't pay a penny, the king liked him even less.

John was always angry when someone didn't like him, but he was especially angry at the king who would reach all the way across the Atlantic Ocean and try to take money from his pocket. Now, when one of his ships landed with paint, paper, tea, glass, and other assorted items, John Hancock was expected to pay a tax on the order.

Already he had troubles enough with his orders. Any man with 20 ships had troubles. Once, for instance, John ordered lemons and when they arrived, they were spoiled. Once a shipment of wine came with the bottles not properly corked. Once he was sent a trunkload of silks of such atrocious colors that no one would buy them. Once he received a watch that didn't keep time. Once a load of oil went overboard. And now England was adding taxes to his troubles!

So, in April, 1768, when the tax inspectors boarded his brig the *Lydia*, loaded with tea and paper, John Hancock wouldn't let them inspect. (John had 10 strong friends with him at the time.)

In May a tax inspector, boarding John's brig the *Liberty*, was shoved into a cabin and the door nailed shut while the crew moved a cargo of taxable wine quietly ashore.

After this, the king put John's name on his list of "Dangerous Americans." In Boston the Tories (those who took the king's side) wrote nasty things about John in the newspaper and drew pictures of him with long ears like a donkey and a conceited grin on his face. John had looked in the mirror often enough to know that his ears weren't long and the cartoons made him madder than ever.

By 1775 it was apparent that there would soon be war between England and the Colonies. On the one hand, English troops stationed in Boston were scouring the countryside for arms hidden by Americans. On the other hand, the people of Massachusetts had cut off all connection with England and had formed their own government. And who was president of this government?

John Hancock, of course.

The king moved John Hancock's name to the top of his Dangerous list and he put a price of 500 pounds on his head.

John was 38 years old now and was engaged to Dolly Quincy, the youngest and prettiest of five Quincy girls. They were to be married in the spring. The north parlor of the Quincy home was ready, its walls newly papered for the occasion with a design of blue cupids shooting blue arrows at red flowers.

But John didn't get to the Quincy home that spring. On April 19 the English troops, marching to Concord to look for American arms, stopped off at Lexington for a battle and so the war started. John, who was hiding in Lexington, had all he could do to keep one step ahead of the English army, but even when he did reach safety, he couldn't go to the room of the blue cupids. Instead he had to hurry off to Philadelphia. John was one of the delegates from Massachusetts to the Continental Congress, a meeting of representatives from all the Colonies to decide what to do about England.

As it turned out, John would probably not have wanted to miss the trip to Philadelphia even for his own wedding. The news of the Lexington battle had spread and all along the way people toasted, dined, escorted, paraded, and cheered the brave delegates from Massachusetts. Such huzzas—mile after mile of huzzas! Outside New York City the delegates were met by a regiment of soldiers, by gentlemen in carriages, gentlemen on horseback, and thousands of gentlemen on foot raising the greatest cloud of dust, John said, that he'd ever seen. At one point the people were so

carried away by excitement that they tried to release John's horses and drag his chariot through the streets themselves. It was a grand parade, John wrote Dolly, "the Carriage of your humble servant of course being the first in the Procession . . . No Person," he added happily, "could possibly be more noticed than myself."

Yet John was to receive even more notice. Two weeks later, in Philadelphia, the members of the Congress, finding themselves suddenly without a president, began looking around for a likely candidate. And whom did they see?

Your humble servant, John Hancock. King George's Number One Enemy.

"We'll show the king what we think of him!" they cried and amid a great round of laughter, they picked John Hancock up bodily and set him in the president's chair where, they voted unanimously, he should stay.

And there he sat every day in his fine clothes, like a gracious host, recognizing first one person and then another, trying to keep everyone happy while he himself remained the center of attention. He had other duties, of course. He had many letters to write, and when legislation was passed, he had to sign his name.

John Hancock loved to sign his name. Over the years he had tried different styles of writing. Sometimes he simply underlined his name.

John Hancock

Sometimes he tried putting a curlicue beneath it.

Jno Hancock

Sometimes he tried both underlining and curlicueing.

John Hancock

But when John Hancock became president of the Second Continental Congress, he began writing his name bigger and with greater flourish. Huge commanding *J*'s, long wavy-tailed *k*'s. Underlinings that streamed back and forth; curlicues with bars through them.

John Hancock Presidt

John had plenty of practice writing. He signed his name to orders for food, gunpowder, and clothing; to directions for moving troops, building forts, and catching spies. But never did he sign more boldly than he did one day in the summer of 1776.

All spring the members of Congress had been arguing about whether Americans should declare their independence. Some said, *No, not yet;* some said, *Yes, now*. But not until late on the rainy afternoon of July 2 did they agree that yes, Americans should declare. It took two more days to agree on exactly how the Declaration of Independence (prepared by Thomas Jefferson) should be worded and another month for the final copy to be drafted on parchment for the members to sign.

John Hancock signed first. He flipped back his lace cuffs, dipped his quill pen in the silver inkstand on the desk, and he wrote large. He was, after all, making history. If America won the war, he would be honored as the first Signer; if America lost, he would be the first to be hanged for treason. John swished and swirled his curlicues.

"There!" he said. "George the Third can read *that* without his spectacles. Now he can double his reward for my head."

For much of the war John lived in comfort. He and Dolly were married in the summer of 1775 (not among the blue cupids, but at a friend's house in Connecticut), and although they did not have 54 windows, their house was large and roomy. John ate as well, drank as well, dressed as well as he ever had.

But there were times when the war came so close that Congress had to move out of Philadelphia and John had to give up some of his comforts. Occasionally he had to eat without a tablecloth. Once he was so cold that he had to borrow two blankets. Once he was without a candle snuffer and complained that he had to use common scissors to put out his candle. Once he was forced to dip out his gravy with a pewter teaspoon until someone took pity and lent him a large silver spoon. Once he ate turkey that was so tough that he broke a tooth. "I wish I could do better," he wrote after some of these hardships, "but we must Ruff it."

There were other times, however, when John lived with more splendor than most people thought proper. Once, in the midst of the war he turned a trip from Philadelphia to Boston into a private parade. Riding in a fancy chariot that had been taken from a pirate ship, John was accompanied by four servants dressed in fancy uniforms. Twenty-five horsemen with drawn sabers rode before him; twenty-five more horsemen with drawn sabers rode behind. He was only traveling, he thought, in a manner that fitted his position, but others said he was peacocking about like an Oriental prince.

But for all the attention that John Hancock received presiding over Congress, he always imagined that he would receive more attention fighting battles. He had once even hoped to be commander in chief of the army. Indeed, he had expected it. When the day came for Congress to elect a commander, and when John Adams rose to make the first nomination, John Hancock was so sure he would hear his name that he arranged his face accordingly. As it turned out, he had to rearrange his face fast.

John Adams nominated George Washington and Samuel Adams seconded the nomination. John Hancock never felt the same about the Adamses after that, but in the summer of 1778 he did at last have a chance to fight a battle.

John thought it would be a short and easy battle. All that had to be done was to drive a garrison of 6,000 English soldiers out of Rhode Island. To do this there would be a squadron of the French fleet, 5,000 soldiers from the Continental Army, and 5,000 New England soldiers under the command of—who else?

Major General John Hancock of the Massachusetts Militia. John looked forward to putting on his new blue uniform, getting on his horse, galloping into battle, and collecting his huzzas. But nothing went right. The sound of cannon gave him a headache. He forgot to take along a favorite pair of boots. It rained, and it was hard for him to feel like a hero when he was wet. A storm at sea crippled the French fleet and sent it to Boston for repairs. Three thousand men deserted. In short, the Rhode Island expedition was a disaster without a single huzza. John Hancock said he had exerted himself to the extent of his "slender constitution," and he packed up and went home.

Meanwhile, in Boston, officers of the French fleet waiting for their ships to be repaired, were feeling unappreciated. After all, they had come a long way to help America, yet no one was entertaining them. Some people were even criticizing them for leaving Rhode Island in too much of a hurry. What was needed was a host to keep the French happy—and who was Boston's Number One Host?

John Hancock, of course. He took off his general's uniform, put on his velvets and satins, and invited 30 French

officers to breakfast. The next morning, however, instead of 30 officers, 120 officers arrived. When Dolly saw them coming, she ran to the kitchen, handed out jugs, vases, bowls, pitchers, and mugs to the servants and sent them scurrying to the Common to milk the cows. No matter whose cows, she said; they were to milk them all. When they returned, she sent them to the neighbors to borrow cake, and when the cake was grabbed by the officers as it was being brought in the door, Dolly ordered the servants to hide the cake in buckets and cover them with napkins.

The French couldn't seem to get enough to eat. Twelve pounds of butter were used at that breakfast and all the cows on the Common were drained dry. One officer drank 17 cups of tea; others went into the garden and picked the fruit trees bare.

Still, John Hancock was determined to keep the French happy and he went on entertaining them for the six weeks they were there. When he couldn't find enough food in Boston, he sent to Providence.

"Chickens," he said. "Ducks, geese, ham, partridges, and especially butter—do you have any? Are there mellons or peaches? Turkey?"

At one time there were 150 live turkeys shut up in the coachhouse. The poor cook was so busy night and day picking feathers that once to John's embarrassment she sent a turkey that hadn't been picked clean to the table. But the French had food and in the end John had his victory—not on the battlefield as he had expected, but at the dinner table, where he was at his best. When the French left Boston, they huzzaed John in French. "Bravo!" they shouted. "Vive John Hancock! Bravo! Bravo!"

The last battle of the war was fought in 1781, but before this the states began to set up their governments in a permanent form. In 1780 Massachusetts adopted its constitution and held an election. And who became the first governor?

His Excellency, John Hancock, Esquire. He won 9,475 votes out of a total of 10,383. And when he took office, cannons fired, bells rang, parades marched, crowds huzzaed, and the sun shone. Parties went on for weeks.

Now that he was governor, John ordered a new coach, 6 dozen pewter dishes with his crest engraved on every dish, oval serving plates for the fish dinners he gave for 50 or 60 people every Saturday night, new curtains, new cushions, 12 "stuff-back" chairs, a sofa, carpets, and a silver urn. John wore buttons of solid gold and put gold lace on his hats; the saddle cloth of Dolly's pony was embroidered with silver thread. Indeed, John Hancock lived in such splendor that he was often called "King Hancock" behind his back. And like many kings, he had a court jester to keep him amused. There was in Boston a hatter named Balch who was famous for his jokes, and so when John went driving, he took Balch with him. It was said that when the governor approached, people could hear him laughing before they could see the coach.

41

John Hancock was elected governor 11 times. Regularly
he threatened to retire but people said this was only because
he wanted to be coaxed to stay. Yet being governor wasn't
everything. He often wanted more. Indeed, he might have
liked to use that old wishing stone, but he was a governor
now; he didn't even dress himself. So how would he look
running around in circles on the Common? And it was not
the sort of thing a man could ask a servant to do for him.
Still, John had his wishes.

In 1789, when he was 52 years old, he wished very much to be elected Vice President of the United States. But he received only 4 of the 69 electoral votes and John Adams was elected instead.

He never stopped wishing for children to survive him. He had had two children: a little girl, Lydia, who lived only a few months, and a son, George Washington Hancock, who was killed when he fell and hit his head while trying out a new pair of ice skates. George was 9 years old at the time.

And John would, if he could, have wished away his enemies. As popular as he was with the common people, he had enemies. They criticized him for spending too much money, for being a show off, and for changing his mind so often or for not making it up at all. John hated to take sides; after all, he wanted both sides and everyone to like him.

Certainly John would have wished for good health. But he had headaches that were so bad that he couldn't bear for anyone (except himself) to make the slightest noise. Once, a servant dropping a plate sent John into a tantrum; once, a maid, taking out her paper hair curlers in the hall outside his door, made a rustle and John screamed for quiet.

As his health failed, John's handwriting became shaky.

Most troublesome was his gout. John's legs would swell
and become so painful that he had to wrap them up in yards
and yards of red flannel and if he wanted to move, he had
to be carried. Some people said John used his gout as an
excuse. If he didn't want to make up his mind, he wrapped
up his legs and said he was sick. He seldom seemed to miss
a parade or a party.

Certainly he never wanted to miss the general review of military companies that was held every October on Boston Common. It was one of the best parades of the year, with fifes playing, drums beating, guns shooting, and at the end, of course, plenty of huzzas. In October, 1793, John planned to put up a huge tent where he would entertain the officers after the review. But off and on all fall John was sick and on the morning of the review he died. When the news was

announced on the Common, the fifers put away their fifes, the drummers their drums, and all quietly went home.

The funeral was held six days later. At noon 20,000 people gathered on the Common to march four abreast in a procession a mile and a half long to the burying ground. There had never been such a long procession in Boston. But, after all, there had never been a John Hancock before, either.

Notes from the Author

Page

7 John Hancock was born January 23, 1737.

20 The English seized the *Liberty,* towed it into the harbor, and moored it under the guns of their armed frigate the *Romney.* This made the people of Boston so angry that they took the chief tax collector's boat out of the water and burned it on the Common.

21 Pound = a unit of English money.

21 John Adams thought that in later years people would celebrate July 2, the day Congress decided that independence would be declared. On July 4 the actual wording was agreed upon and John Hancock signed this document without any ceremony, just as he would any piece of legislation. His name and that of his secretary were the only ones that appeared on the Declaration until the official parchment copy was signed by him and the other members on August 2.

30 Ruff. In Colonial times spelling had not become as standardized as it is today. Even educated people often spelled words as they saw fit. (Notice on page 38 how John spells "mellon.")

39 Vive John Hancock = Long live John Hancock.

42 After the years in Philadelphia Samuel Adams was one of John's enemies, but in 1789 when John was elected governor for the ninth time, Samuel Adams was elected lieutenant governor, and they became friends again. They were inaugurated in twin suits that John provided.